AF593546

Living
With Loss

kevin
mayhew

In memory of my father,
so much loved in life,
so much missed in death

First published in 2005 by

KEVIN MAYHEW LTD
Buxhall, Stowmarket, Suffolk, IP14 3BW
E-mail: info@kevinmayhewltd.com

9 8 7 6 5 4 3 2 1 0

ISBN 1 84417 367 4
Catalogue No. 1500771

Designed by Chris Coe

Printed and bound in China

Contents

Introduction

Few things are worse than losing a loved one. We may have empathised with others in their time of loss and done our best to prepare ourselves for the moment when bereavement strikes us in turn, but when that finally comes, the intensity of the emotional rollercoaster we find ourselves experiencing can still take us by surprise. First and foremost, of course, there is grief, an almost devastating sense of loss as we realise that, in this life at least, we are irrevocably parted from somebody who has been integral to our lives – never again to see their face, hear their voice or share their company. Alongside that comes a host of other feelings: for some, guilt; for others, panic; for others again, anger; for others still, a crisis of faith – and so we could go on. How do we express those emotions? How can we deal with them in such a way as to use them constructively rather than allow them to eat away within? How do we make sense of death and our own continuing life? For the Christian such questions are as pressing as any.

Of course, I do not have all the answers – far from it – and this book is not intended in any way to suggest otherwise. It represents rather my own attempt to wrestle with the issues and trauma surrounding bereavement, offered in the hope that something within its pages may prove of consolation, help or encouragement to others. Why though are the prayers presented in the form of poetry? The answer is very simple. For me, verse – and rhyming verse in particular – is able to express things in a way that prose alone cannot quite match. The rhythm carries the reader along and the rhyme gives a sense of completeness and final resolution, the two in tandem making the words easy to remember and repeat.

Not, of course, that there is any easy resolution to the experience of losing someone we love. Far from a sense of completeness there is more often a feeling of chilling finality, often made all the worse by the fact that death is taboo, most people preferring to avoid the issue rather than discuss it candidly. The aim of these prayers, or poems – call them what you will – is to provide a way of opening up before God, honestly pouring out the emotions bereavement brings, in the hope that, through doing so, we might discover something of the hope, comfort, peace and strength he longs to impart. To put it more simply, they are offered to help you pray.

Nick Fawcett

The Pain of Loss

Glory to God, the Father not only of Jesus Christ our Lord but also of all mercies – a God full of consolation, who offers us solace in whatever troubles we are facing.

2 Corinthians 1:3-4a

I thought that I was ready,
prepared to say goodbye,
aware death waits for no one;
that each of us must die.
I knew loss would be painful,
whatever time it came;
that life from that point onwards
would never be the same,
but even though I feared it,
deep down I dared to hope
that when bereavement hit me
I'd confidently cope.

How different, Lord, the truth
now I'm facing it for real,
how deep the sense of heartbreak
and hopelessness I feel,
how bittersweet the memories,
how bleak the future seems,
how futile all my hoping
and fragile all my dreams.
A world, which seemed so stable,
now whirls in disarray,
for part of me is missing,
for ever plucked away.
Lord, meet me in my sorrow
and grant the help I crave,
remind me of your promise
of life beyond the grave.
Speak of your loving purpose
and help me as I grieve,
to hear your words of comfort
and truly to believe.

Facing the Truth

My eyes grow weary as I look
for the fulfilment of your promise.
'When will you bring me comfort?'
I find myself asking.
Psalm 119:82

Lord, I scarcely dare to face
the pain I feel inside,
running rather from the truth
that one I love has died.
Though I know I need to grieve
before the wounds can heal,
I'm afraid of letting loose
the sense of loss I feel –
scared that I'll be overwhelmed,
engulfed and swept along,
the pent-up tide too fierce to stem,
the memories too strong.

Teach me, Lord, to open up
and bring my fears to you,
trusting you will still the storm
and help me work them through.
So, in time, may I look back
with thanks across the years,
thinking of the days I shared
with joy instead of tears;
confident that though, for now,
death forces us apart,
those I love are with me still,
alive within my heart.

Letting Go

**The souls of the faithful are in God's hands,
pain no longer able to touch them.
Those who know no better believe them
to have died, and consider death to be a tragedy,
their parting to have robbed them of life, but
they are at peace. The faithful live forevermore
and the sovereign God will take care of them.**

Wisdom of Solomon 3:1-3

I saw my loved one suffer,
each moment touched with pain,
the body slowly failing,
too weak to take the strain.
I knew each day brought testing,
more cruel than words can tell,
until life, once so special,
became a living hell:
the only thing that mattered,
at last to be at peace;

the only goal to strive for,
to somehow find release;
no reason still to struggle
or cause to fear the end;
an enemy no longer,
death beckoned as a friend.
At last the pain is over –
it falls to me instead –
Lord, may that knowledge help me
to face the days ahead.

The Shadow of Death

Even though I walk through a valley
overshadowed by the darkness of death
I will not fear any evil, for you will be there
beside me, always ready with your staff
and crook to offer comfort.
Psalm 23:4

I've lost one who I loved, Lord,
more precious than can be,
who brought life joy and meaning,
and meant the world to me.
Each day I yearn for comfort,
yet cannot find relief –
the smile I wear in public,
a mask to hide my grief –
for all we shared is over,
its joy beyond recall;
a cloud obscures my vision
and overshadows all.

And yet, in scattered moments,
I glimpse another side –
although for now we're parted
not everything has died:
the empathy between us,
the love that freely flowed,
the happiness and laughter,
the time and care bestowed,
all these have helped to bring me
to where I am today,
each one a priceless treasure
that death can't pluck away.
So when I'm feeling wretched,
dejected and bereft,
Lord, help me to remember
how much there still is left;
to recognise more fully
the blessings I've enjoyed:
their legacy continues
and will not be destroyed.

Honestly Remembered

Come what may, love makes allowances, keeps faith, sees the best, continues undiminished. It cannot be extinguished.
1 Corinthians 13:7-8a

Lord, help me to remember
the person that I knew,
not some idealised portrait
no longer ringing true.
Remind me of each aspect,
the special and mundane,
the failings and the virtues,
the beautiful and plain,
the triumphs and the failures,
the happy and the sad,
the folly and the wisdom,
the good times and the bad,
the moments of contentment
and days of dark despair,

the words that spoke of anger
and deeds that spoke of care,
the laughter and the sorrow,
the pleasure and the pain,
the hopes that found fulfilment,
the dreams that proved in vain.
Not every trait was perfect,
nor every feature good,
not everything between us
worked out quite as it should,
but all these points together
combined in such a way
to craft one far more precious
than words can ever say –
a person who I value
for everything they've been,
and one I'll go on loving
for what they'll always mean.

Getting By

Tears may continue through the hours of darkness, but joy will come with the dawn.
Psalm 30:5b

How can I cope with this pain inside,
this ache within my heart?
How can I deal with the tears I hide?
Where can I even start?
When will despair loose its stranglehold
and let me find some peace?
When will I laugh as I did of old?
When will the hurting cease?
Part of my life is a part no more,
suddenly gone for good.
Nothing can be as it was before,
much though I wish it could.
Strengthen me, Lord, in this time of need,
comfort me as I mourn.
Reach out your hand to support and lead;
after the night bring dawn.

New Beginnings

**The enduring love of the Lord never fades,
nor can anything ever exhaust his mercies;
such is his great faithfulness that each morning
they are made new once more.**

Lamentations 3:22-23

Speak of your awesome care, Lord,
that death cannot deny,
your sovereign grace and purpose,
your love that will not die.
Comfort me in my sorrow,
breathe peace within my heart,
remind me of the treasures
you promise to impart:
eternal peace and blessing,
unutterable joy,
contentment and fulfilment
that nothing can destroy.
Remind me, when I need it,
that all is not yet done –
a chapter may be over,
but life has just begun.

Defeat and Victory

**Death has been consumed by victory.
Where is your triumph now, death,
and where is your sting?**
1 Corinthians 15:54b-55

Everything seems diminished,
so much no longer applies;
part of my life feels finished –
death has exacted its prize.
No more will words be spoken,
moments together be shared,
the golden thread is broken
and never can be repaired.

Come, Lord, and grant your healing,
foster contentment anew.
Reach out in love, revealing
all that in time you will do.
Though I may feel forsaken,
bleak though the world might appear,
teach me that I'm mistaken –
show me I've nothing to fear.
Yes, something *is* completed,
but not as so many assume:
death is destroyed, defeated,
life will burst fresh from the tomb!

Faith in Things Unseen

The passing sufferings we endure at the moment are preparing for us an eternal weight of glory beyond measure, because we look beyond this world to one that cannot be seen. What we can see is transient – here today and gone tomorrow. Eternal things are hidden from our sight.

2 Corinthians 4:17-18

I do not know what heaven is,
the where or when or how;
if it's a kingdom yet to come
or all around us now.
I cannot claim to understand
the complex ins and outs –
in fact, along with faith I have
a healthy share of doubts.
So am I whistling in the dark,
just clutching hold of straws,
content to cling to anything
that soothes and reassures?
Is dread of facing up to truth
the root of my belief;
this hope of mine some cosy way
of coping with my grief?

It's true I'll never prove that life
continues after death,
to claim that it is otherwise
is just a waste of breath.
That one day we will rise again,
not simply turn to dust,
cannot be shown by argument,
but has to rest on trust.
Our faith in what God holds in store
goes deeper than the mind,
not solely based on reasoning
but of another kind:
its source the one who died, yet lives
and walks with us each day,
whose gracious love encircles us
each step along the way.
In him I find a certainty
on which I can depend,
for love like this, so full, so free,
can surely never end.

The Price of Loving

There is a season for everything –
a time to be born and a time to die,
a time to plant and a time to uproot . . .
a time to cry and a time to laugh,
a time to grieve and a time to dance.
Ecclesiastes 3:1a, 2, 4

I couldn't understand, Lord,
how you could let it be.
Despite my search for answers,
I simply couldn't see.
Why do we have to suffer?
Why do you let us die?
Why does so much deny you
and give your love the lie?
I've wrestled with such questions
and still not worked them out,
the best that I can offer
a blend of faith and doubt.
Yet in this combination,
this balance of the two,
I'm coming, Lord, to wonder
if there you give a clue.

For just as talk of darkness
demands we speak of light,
so there can be no morning
unless there's also night,
no laughter without sorrow,
no pleasure without pain,
no goodness without evil,
no sunshine without rain.
Unless we have the second
we cannot have the first,
the 'best' has little meaning
unless there is a 'worst'.
Is that what you are saying
as now I grieve in turn?
Is this the vital lesson
you're asking me to learn?
Beginnings go with endings –
I've loved and I have lost.
I've shared such special blessing –
now I must bear the cost.

Thanks for the Memories

**The everlasting God is your eternal home;
his loving arms will support you for ever.**
Deuteronomy 33:27

There's so much I wanted to say, Lord,
so much I wanted to do,
all kinds of hopes left unrealised,
dreams that I'll never see through:
news I would once have related,
deeds showing how much I cared,
love I intended to speak of –
all can no longer be shared.

Help me to face my emotions,
deal with the sorrow I feel,
cope with the pain of remembering,
such that, in time, these might heal.
Teach me to look back with gladness,
happy in spite of the tears,
grateful for wonderful memories,
joy spanning so many years.
So may I find consolation
when I feel lost and alone,
able to grieve with a smile,
thankful for all I have known.

Thanksgiving for a Parent

You have transformed my grief into celebration, clothing me with gladness rather than funeral attire, such that instead of keeping quiet my soul sings out in praise. Lord God, I would offer you heartfelt thanks, now and always.

Psalm 30:11-12

In the sorrow that I'm feeling
as I try to take things in;
though my broken heart is reeling,
and my mind is in a spin;
call to mind, Lord, all the pleasure
that I've shared across the years –
moments I will always treasure
with a smile as well as tears:

hands that nurtured and provided,
bandaged wounds and helped me grow;
words that comforted and guided,
teaching much of what I know;
times of happiness and laughter,
deeds that spoke of love and care,
days that I'll recall long after –
– such a privilege to share.
Lord, although a weight of sadness,
leaves me grieving and distressed,
deep within there's also gladness
for I've been so richly blessed.

Comfort for Those Who Mourn

Blessed are those who grieve,
for they will receive comfort.
Matthew 5:4

'Happy are those who weep', you said;
'happy are they who mourn' –
weeping will turn to joy instead,
pleasure will be reborn;
death will not have the final word,
darkness not win the day,
laughter will once again be heard,
tears will be wiped away.
Help me to trust, Lord, though I grieve,
show me your word is true.
Give me the courage to believe
joy still can shoot anew.
Comfort me in the pain I feel,
order the storm to cease,
reach out in love to help and heal,
come now, and grant your peace.

The Promise of New Life

Nothing that you sow can spring to life unless it dies first. For whatever you plant is transitory, but what rises from this will never die.

1 Corinthians 15:36b, 42b

Lord, autumn leaves are falling,
the trees will soon be bare;
a multitude of endings
surround me everywhere.
So much that bloomed so brightly
now seems a world away,
its glory but a memory,
supplanted by decay.
Yet, hidden in the darkness,
beneath the silent earth,
already shoots are forming –
a promise of new birth.
And, softly, you are saying,
to those with ears to hear,
though death for now brings sorrow,
keep hope and do not fear.
Yes, life may seem extinguished,
but days to come will bring
beginnings after endings,
in place of winter, spring.

A Love That Conquers Death

I saw a new heaven and earth in which God will dwell with his people. He will wipe every tear from their eyes. There will be no more death nor any mourning, crying or pain. Such former things will all have passed away.

Revelation 21:1a, 3b-4

Give me greater faith, Lord,
in your love that conquers death,
a love that keeps on burning
beyond our dying breath,
a purpose that continues
unchanged forevermore,
and when this life is over
still holds the best in store.
Speak of the special future
you want us to enjoy,

the blessings of your kingdom
that nothing can destroy;
a realm of awesome beauty
where joy will never cease,
no hatred there or warfare,
but everlasting peace;
a place of hope and healing
where tears are washed away,
and those oppressed by darkness
will bask in endless day.
Although my heart is heavy,
although I need to grieve,
Lord, nurture trust within me
and help me to believe.
Remind me truth is greater
than I can comprehend:
however much it seems so,
the grave is not the end.

We'll Meet Again

With the Lord's authority, I tell you this: those of us who are alive, left waiting for his coming, will not be given preference over those who have died. Rather, those of us left alive will mysteriously be caught up with them into the heavens to meet him, to be by his side for ever.

1 Thessalonians 4:15, 17

The time had come, a time to die –
with heavy heart I said goodbye.
The world felt bleak, my mind was numb,
for what I feared to see had come.
Someone so dear was dead and gone,
yet Lord, through you, life carries on –
I don't know how, I don't when,
but, by your grace, we'll meet again.